Christmas Peace

Holiday Solos for Intermediate Piano

Arrangements and Music by
Pam Turner

www.pamturnerpiano.com

Copyright ℗ 2018 Pam Turner and Pam Turner Piano (ASCAP)
The music, text, design, and graphics in this publication are protected
by copyright law. Unauthorized duplication is prohibited.

Christmas Peace
Holiday Solos for Intermediate Piano

Arrangements & Music by Pam Turner

Copyright ® 2018 Pam Turner and Pam Turner Piano (ASCAP)
Distributed by Pam Turner Piano

All rights reserved. The arrangements, text and graphics in this publication are protected by copyright law. No part of this work may be duplicated or reprinted without the prior consent of the author.

ISBN 978-1790579617

Pam Turner Piano

www.pamturnerpiano.com

Christmas Peace

Holiday Solos for Intermediate Piano

Ave Maria. 1

Gesù Bambino. 6

O Holy Night. 11

O Come, All Ye Faithful. 16

In the Bleak Midwinter. 19

Still, Still, Still. 23

The First Noel. 27

What Child Is This. 31

Ode to Joy. 37

Canon in D. 41

Silent Night. 45

Hark! The Herald Angels Sing 49

Of the Father's Love Begotten. 53

Peace. 57

www.pamturnerpiano.com

Ave Maria

J. S. Bach/Charles Gounod
Arr. Pam Turner

Flowing gracefully, in two

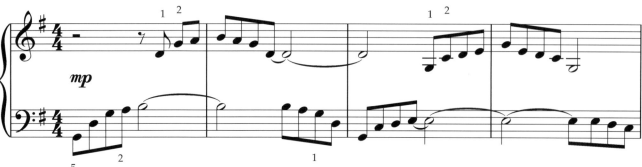

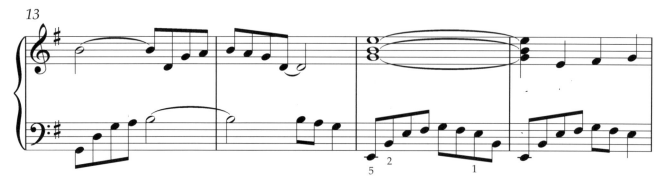

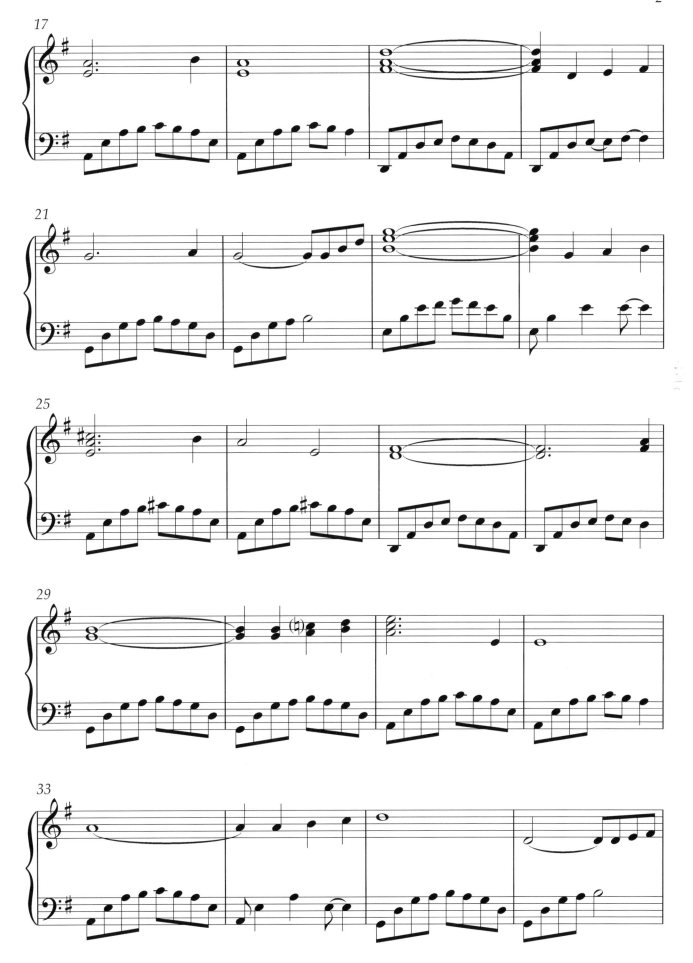

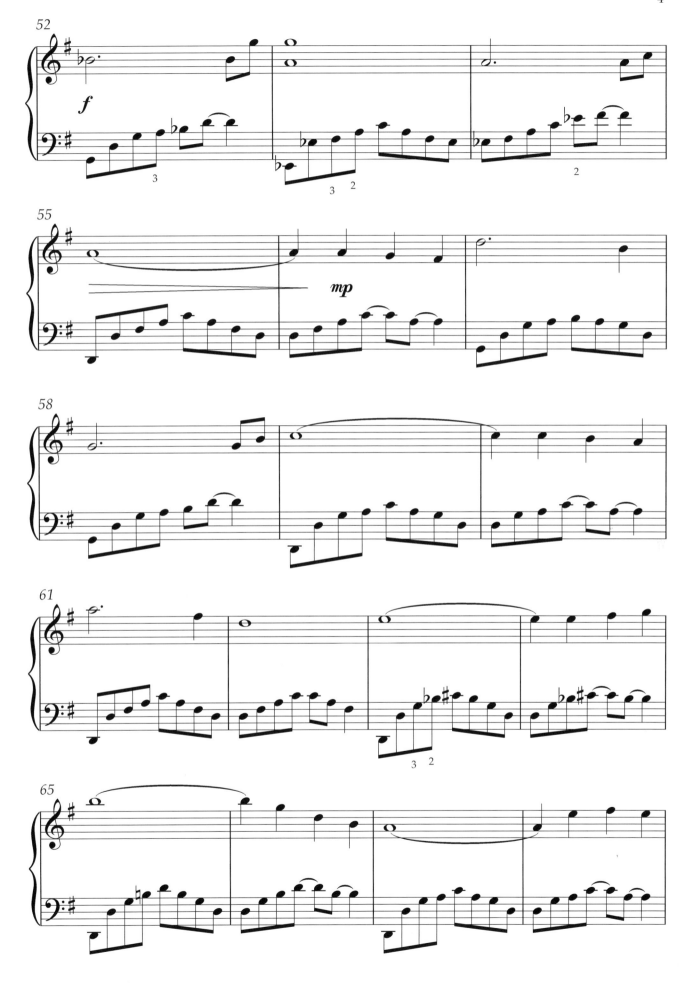

Gesù Bambino

Pietro Yon
Arr. Pam Turner

O Holy Night

Adolphe Adam
Arr. Pam Turner

Andante

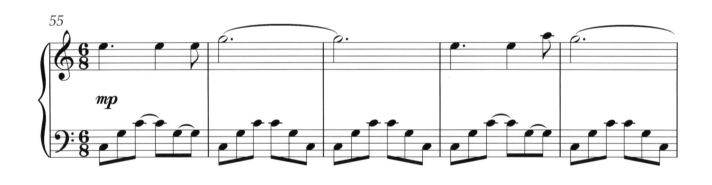

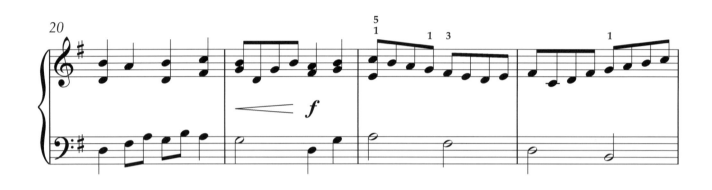

In the Bleak Midwinter

Gustav Holst
Arr. Pam Turner

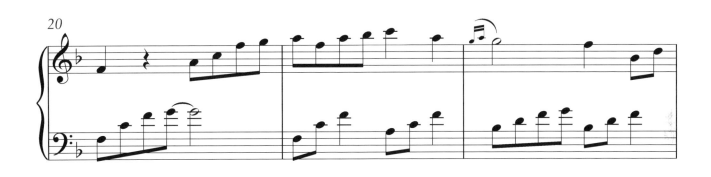

Still, Still, Still

German Traditional
Arr. Pam Turner

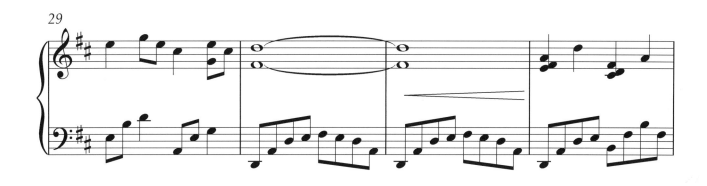

What Child Is This

Traditional English
Arr. Pam Turner

Andante

Copyright 2018 Pam Turner and Pam Turner Piano (ASCAP) | Duplication Prohibited | All Rights Reserved
PamTurnerPiano.com

Ode to Joy

Ludwig van Beethoven
Pam Turner

Triumphantly

Copyright © 2018 Pam Turner and Pam Turner Piano (ASCAP) | Duplication Prohibited | All Rights Reserved
PamTurnerPiano.com

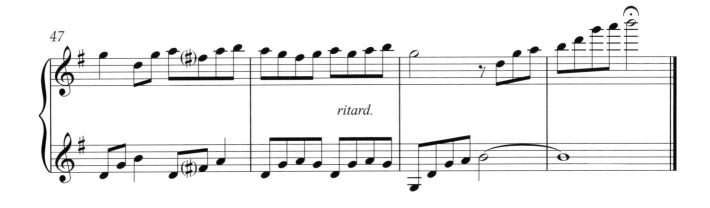

Canon in D

Johann Pachelbel
Arr. Pam Turner

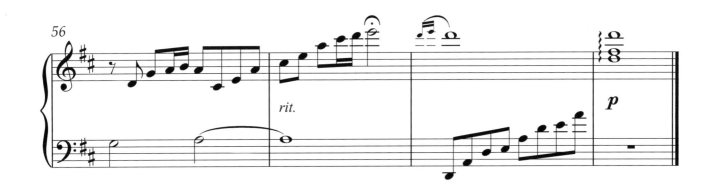

Silent Night

Franz Gruber
Arr. Pam Turner

Andante cantabile

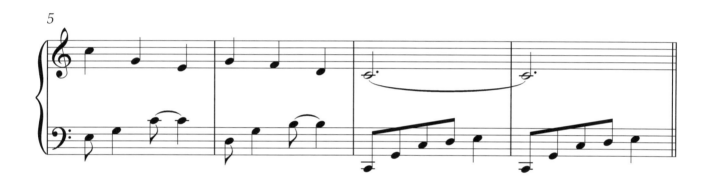

Hark! The Herald Angels Sing

Felix Mendelssohn
Arr. Pam Turner

Moderately

Of the Father's Love Begotten

DIVINUM MYSTERIUM
Plainsong Melody, 13th Century
Arr. Pam Turner

Simply and unhurried ♩=66

Copyright © 2018 Pam Turner and Pam Turner Piano (ASCAP) | Duplication Prohibited | All Rights Reserved
PamTurnerPiano.com

Peace
a meditation on John 14:27

Thoughtfully, with rubato

Pam Turner

Made in United States
Orlando, FL
26 November 2024

54502861R00037